FANTASTIC FACTS ABOUT

BATTLES, WARS AND REVOLUTIONS

Author
Anita Ganeri, Hazel Mary Martell, Brian Williams

Editor
Jane Walker

Design
First Edition

Image Coordination
Ian Paulyn

Production Assistant
Rachel Jones

Index
Jane Parker

Editorial Director
Paula Borton

Design Director
Clare Sleven

Publishing Director
Jim Miles

This is a Parragon Publishing Book

This edition is published in 2001

Parragon Publishing, Queen Street House, 4 Queen Street, Bath BA1 1HE, UK

Copyright Parragon © 2000

Parragon has previously printed this material in 1999 as part of the Factfinder series

2 4 6 8 10 9 7 5 3 1

Produced by Miles Kelly Publishing Ltd
Bardfield Centre, Great Bardfield, Essex CM7 4SL

ISBN 0-75254-880-8

Printed in China

FANTASTIC FACTS ABOUT

BATTLES, WARS AND REVOLUTIONS

p

CONTENTS

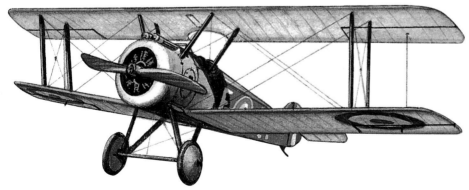

INTRODUCTION

To a large extent, the history of civilization has been shaped by its battles and wars. Here you will encounter warriors and soldiers, kings and politicians through the ages. Find out about civil war in England and America, and about revolutions in China and France. Finally discover the impact of two world wars in the 20th century and how conflict around the globe has affected all our lives.

BATTLES, WARS, AND REVOLUTIONS is a handy reference guide in the *Fascinating Facts* series. Each book has been specially compiled with a collection of stunning illustrations and photographs which bring the subject to life. Hundreds of facts and figures are presented in a variety of interesting ways and time-bars provide information at-a-glance. This unique combination is fun and easy to use and makes learning a pleasure.

VIKING RAIDERS

From the late 700s, bands of Vikings sailed overseas in their longships, landing on the coasts of western Europe. They raided monasteries and towns, carrying off slaves and booty, and seized land. From 865 Vikings from Denmark settled in eastern England. They attacked what is now France, but were bought off with the gift of Normandy in 911. Norwegian Vikings settled in Iceland and Greenland, and landed in North America. Vikings wandered in the markets of Baghdad and Constantinople, bringing back exotic goods to towns such as Jorvik (York) and Dublin.

Viking warrior

Chain-mail tunic

Iron sword

Leather shield

GREENLAND
BAFFIN ISLAND
DENMARK
ICELAND
NORWAY
SWEDEN
Novgorod
LABRADOR
Clontarf
Kiev
GERMANY
FRANCE
Istanbul
SPAIN
Sicily

■ Danish Vikings
■ Norwegian Vikings
■ Swedish Vikings

VIKING TRADE ROUTES
The Vikings traveled by sea and overland to England and Ireland in the west, and as far east as Baghdad and Istanbul.

VIKING INFLUENCE

Many Vikings were peaceful farmers and traders who chose to settle in the new lands, mingling with the local people. In England, King Alfred defeated the invaders, but Viking settlements in eastern England (the Danelaw) left a permanent legacy in customs, laws, place names, and language.

A VIKING RAID

The Vikings were fierce fighters with their favorite iron swords and axes. During an attack, raiders would rush from their longships. The ships could be rowed up rivers and land on beaches, so Vikings often took their enemies by surprise.

Iron ax

The heavy Viking sword was swung in a wide arc.

Oared longship

787 First reported Viking raids on English coast.

795 Vikings begin attacks on Ireland.

834 Vikings raid Dorestad (the Netherlands).

865 Great army of Vikings lands in England.

866 Vikings capture the city of York (Jorvik) in England.

878 English and Vikings agree to divide England between them after Vikings are defeated by King Alfred.

911 Vikings are given Normandy to prevent further attacks on France.

1016–1035 Reign of Canute, Viking king of England, Denmark, and Norway.

1066 Last big Viking attack on England, by Harold Hardrada of Norway.

9

MEDIEVAL CASTLES

 Mighty stone castles dotted the landscape of Europe and the Middle East throughout the Middle Ages. The earliest castles were built by the Norman invaders of England. They were earth mounds, often built on hilltops, with a wooden stockade on top. The castles were soon enlarged and strengthened, with water-filled ditches or moats, stone walls protected by towers, and a massive central stronghold called a keep. Medieval castles were private fortresses for the king or lord who owned them. A castle was also a family home, although early castles were cold and drafty places.

CASTLE DEFENSES

The castle was defended by foot soldiers with spears and bows and by armored knights on horseback. When a castle was attacked, its walls had to be thick enough to withstand catapults, tunnels, and battering rams. The occupants often suffered from starvation or disease, and were forced to surrender.

FEASTING IN THE GREAT HALL
The lord and his followers feasted in the great hall.
The lord and lady sat on a raised dais, and knights
and other members of the household at lower tables.

Musicians

Dancers entertained the feasting family.

10   *Servants carried in food from the kitchen.*

Jousters

JOUSTING KNIGHTS
Jousting was combat on horseback between knights with blunt lances. It was a popular social occasion.

Dogs scavenged for scraps.

500 Byzantines build strong stone castles and walled cities.

800s Arabs build castles in the Middle East and North Africa.

1000s Normans develop the motte (mound) and bailey (enclosure) castle.

1078 William I begins building the Tower of London, England.

1100s Stone keeps become the main castle stronghold.

1180s Castles with square-walled towers are built.

1200s The concentric or ring-wall castle is developed.

1220s Castles with round-walled towers start to be built.

1280s Edward I of England orders a chain of great castles to be built in England and Wales.

1350s Castles made of brick are built in the Netherlands and England.

11

THE CRUSADES

For European Christians, the Crusades were holy wars, with the promise of plunder. For more than 200 years, Christian and Muslim armies fought for control of territory around Jerusalem known as the Holy Land. Jerusalem was a holy city to Jews, Muslims, and Christians but, in 1095, the Muslim Turks banned Christian pilgrims from the city. This angered both the western Christian Church in Rome and the eastern Christian Church in Constantinople. Christians were called upon to free Jerusalem and so launched the First Crusade, or war of the cross.

Steep ramparts

A Crusader knight

ATTACK!
Once Crusaders had conquered lands, they built strong castles to defend them.

Battering rams broke down walls.

A Muslim warrior

SUCCESS AND FAILURE

The Crusades inspired stories of bravery and honor. Crusaders had to be tough to endure difficult conditions on their journey. In 1099 the army of the First Crusade captured Jerusalem. Yet none of the later crusades matched this initial success, and the Crusaders failed to win back the Holy Land.

Giant catapults threw balls of flaming tar.

Boiling oil was poured on attackers.

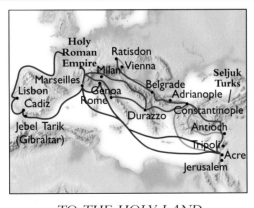

TO THE HOLY LAND

This map shows the different route to Jerusalem taken by the First Crusade (blue), the Second Crusade (yellow), and the Third Crusade (red).

1096 First Crusade is called by Pope Urban II.

1099 The Crusaders defeat the Turks and capture Jerusalem.

1147 Second Crusade sets out.

1187 Muslim leader Saladin captures Jerusalem.

1189 Third Crusade is led by Frederick I Barbarossa of the Holy Roman Empire, Philip II of France, and Richard I of England.

1202 Fourth Crusade attacks Egypt.

1221 Fifth Crusade fights the Sultan of Egypt.

1228 The Sixth Crusade ends when Muslims hand over Jerusalem.

1244 Muslims retake Jerusalem.

1249 Seventh Crusade is led by King Louis IX of France.

1270 Eighth Crusade also led by Louis. He and many of his men die of plague in Tunis.

13

THE MONGOL EMPIRE

In the 1200s, Mongol armies sent a shockwave of fear around Asia and Europe, conquering a vast area of land that formed the largest empire in history.

The Mongols were nomads living on the plains of central Asia. In 1206, Chief Temujin brought all the tribes under his rule and was proclaimed Genghis Khan, meaning lord of all.

WANDERING NOMADS
The Mongols searched for fresh grassland for their herds, carrying their portable felt homes, called yurts, with them.

WARRIORS ON HORSEBACK
Mongol warriors fought on horseback. They controlled their horses with their feet, leaving their hands free to shoot bows and hurl spears.

Bow

Spear

Mongol soldiers were expert archers.

THE WORLD'S LARGEST EMPIRE
Although ruthless in battle, Genghis Khan kept peace
in his empire. It stretched from the River Danube in
the west to the Pacific shores of Asia in the east.

MONGOL CONQUESTS

The Mongols quickly conquered the Persian Empire. They continued their attacks after Genghis Khan died and, in 1237, a Mongol army led by Batu Khan, one of Genghis's sons, invaded Russia. Western Europe was saved only when the Mongols turned homeward on the death of Ogodai Khan in 1241. Enemies feared the Mongols' speed and ferocity in battle. In victory, the Mongols were usually merciless, slaughtering people and plundering treasure. Yet they ruled their empire fairly if sternly.

1206 Temujin becomes chief of all the Mongols, taking the name Genghis Khan.

1215 Beijing, capital of China, is taken by the Mongols.

1217 The Mongols control all China and Korea.

1219 The Mongols attack the empire of Khwarezm (Persia and Turkey).

1224 Mongol armies invade Russia, Poland, and Hungary.

1227 Genghis Khan dies.

1229 Genghis's son, Ogodai, becomes khan.

1237 Mongol army known as the Golden Horde invades northern Russia.

1241 Ogodai dies and his armies pull back from Europe.

KUBLAI KHAN AND CHINA

Kublai Khan, grandson of Genghis Khan, became leader of the Mongols in 1260. His armies moved from the windswept steppes of central Asia to overthrow the Song Dynasty in China, and by 1279 he controlled most of this vast country. At this time, China was the world's most sophisticated, technologically advanced country. The new Mongol emperor moved his capital to Beijing, taking care to maintain many aspects of Chinese culture. Chinese silks, porcelain, and other luxuries astonished travelers from Europe and Africa. After Kublai Khan's death, the Mongol Empire declined and had largely broken up by the mid–1300s.

ALONG THE SILK ROAD
Merchants traveled in caravans for protection against bandits. From China, they followed the Silk Road across mountains and deserts to the markets of the Middle East.

Camels laden with Chinese goods.

Travelers rested at caravanserai, or rest stations.

MARCO POLO (1256–1323)
The Italian explorer Marco Polo toured China in the service of Kublai Khan.

A SOPHISTICATED NATION

After visiting Kublai Khan's court, Marco Polo wrote in praise of Chinese cities, China's fine postal system, and its paper money. The Chinese had discovered technologies such as paper-making. Other inventions included the magnetic compass and exploding gunpowder rockets.

EARLY PAPER

The Chinese began making paper in about 105. They used hemp or tree bark for fiber. Later, they mashed rags or old rope into pulp.

Pulp was spread on mesh trays to dry into sheets.

1216 Kublai Khan is born.

1260 Kublai is elected Great Khan of the Mongols.

1271 Marco Polo sets out from Venice for China.

1274 Kublai Khan sends an army to invade Japan, but it is driven back by a storm.

1276 Mongols defeat the Song fleet near Guangzhou.

1279 Kublai Khan rules all China.

1294 Kublai Khan dies.

1368 Mongols are driven from China by Ming forces.

1395 Tamerlane, a descendant of Genghis Khan, invades large parts of southern Russia.

1398 Tamerlane invades Delhi, India.

1405 Tamerlane dies.

THE HUNDRED YEARS WAR

Edward III became king of England in 1327. He
believed he also had a claim to the French throne so
in 1337, he declared war on France. War between
England and France lasted on and off until 1453.
Edward's forces won a sea battle and two great land victories at
Crécy and Poitiers, but were driven back by the French king
Charles V. In 1360 Edward gave up his claim to the French throne
in return for land.

*Soldiers fought with a
longbow, primitive cannon,
and crossbow.*

The English hoped Joan of Arc's death would end French resistance.

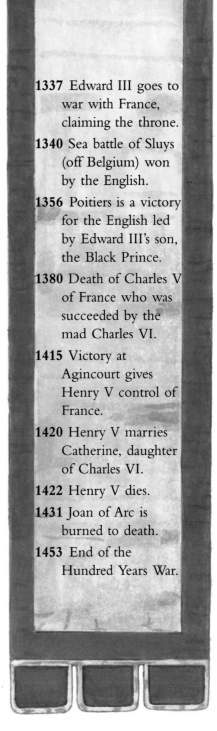

1337 Edward III goes to war with France, claiming the throne.

1340 Sea battle of Sluys (off Belgium) won by the English.

1356 Poitiers is a victory for the English led by Edward III's son, the Black Prince.

1380 Death of Charles V of France who was succeeded by the mad Charles VI.

1415 Victory at Agincourt gives Henry V control of France.

1420 Henry V marries Catherine, daughter of Charles VI.

1422 Henry V dies.

1431 Joan of Arc is burned to death.

1453 End of the Hundred Years War.

Years of truce followed until the English king Henry V renewed his claim to the throne in 1414. He led his troops to France, where they defeated a much larger French army at Agincourt in 1415. To make peace Henry then married the French king's daughter, but he died in 1422 before his baby son could become king of France. The fighting continued as the French were inspired by a peasant girl named Joan of Arc (1412-1431). She fought until the English caught her and burned her at the stake. Under the weak rule of Henry VI, the English lost ground and by 1453, they had lost all French territory except Calais.

EMPIRES OF THE SUN

Two civilizations reached their peak during the early 1500s—the Aztecs in Central America and the Incas in South America. The empires of both civilizations eventually fell to Spanish rule. The Aztecs were fierce warriors whose empire stretched across Mexico. They were skilled sculptors, poets, musicians, and engineers, but in 1521 they lost their empire to Spanish treasure-seekers.

THE END OF AN EMPIRE
The Spanish were vastly outnumbered in their battles with the Incas. But the Europeans had horses and guns, both new to the Incas. When the Inca ruler Atahualpa was killed, the leaderless Inca armies were quickly defeated.

Spanish soldier on horseback.

The Inca armies were weak after seven years of civil war.

A sacrificial knife

The warriors of the Aztec ruling class wore decorative headdresses. These were made from the tail feathers of the quetzal, a sacred bird.

THE INCAS OF PERU

From the mountains of Peru, the god-emperor of the Incas ruled a highly organized empire. The Inca ruler Pachacuti and his successors increased the empire to include parts of Chile, Bolivia, and Ecuador. The Incas built stone cities, such as their capital at Cuzco, and fine roads for trade. In the 1530s a small Spanish expedition under Francisco Pizarro arrived to seek gold in South America. The Spanish killed the emperor Atahualpa and defeated his armies, causing the empire to fall.

1325 The Aztec capital of Tenochtitlan is founded.

1438 Inca Empire starts, under Pachacuti.

1440–1469 Reign of Montezuma I.

1450–1500 The Inca Empire is extended into modern-day Bolivia, Chile, Ecuador and Colombia.

1519 Hernando Cortés leads Spanish soldiers into Tenochtitlan. Montezuma welcomes them, believing Cortés is the god Quetzalcoatl.

1520 The Aztecs rise up against the Spanish. Montezuma dies.

1521 Cortés captures Tenochtitlan, ending the Aztec Empire.

1527 Death of the Inca emperor Huayna Capac; civil war starts between his sons.

1532 Francisco Pizarro, with 167 soldiers, attacks Inca forces and captures Cuzco.

MING CHINA

In 1368 a Buddhist monk named Ming Hong Wu founded the Ming Dynasty, which ruled China for almost 300 years. Under Hong Wu, China enjoyed peace and prosperity. He made Chinese society more equal by abolishing slavery, redistributing land, and demanding higher taxes from the rich. With a strong army, China reasserted its power over its neighbors. The Ming Dynasty was also a period of great artistic creativity.

JAPANESE INVADERS
Chinese soldiers fight against invading Japanese samurai. In the 1590s the Japanese tried to invade Korea, an ally of the Chinese.

Japanese samurai warrior

Chinese soldier on horseback

An arrow fired from a powerful bow could pierce a wooden shield.

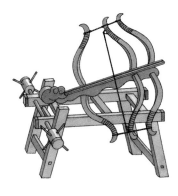

A CHINESE CROSSBOW
A powerful artillery crossbow like this could fire an arrow up to 650 feet (200 m).

CONTACT WITH OUTSIDERS

China's first contacts with European traders began in the 1500s, when Portuguese ships arrived. Western traders were eager to buy Chinese porcelain and silk and a new drink, tea, which first reached Europe in 1610. The Chinese had seldom looked far beyond their borders and after the mid–1500s the government banned voyages overseas.

THE FORBIDDEN CITY
From 1421, the Ming emperors lived inside the Forbidden City in Beijing, a huge complex of palaces, temples, and parks into which no foreigner was admitted.

1368 The Ming Dynasty is founded.

1398 Death of the first Ming emperor, Hong Wu.

1405–1433 Admiral Zheng He leads seven voyages to explore India and East Africa.

1421 The capital moves from Nanjing to Beijing.

1514 Portuguese traders arrive in China, followed by the Dutch in 1522.

1551 Chinese government bans voyages beyond Chinese waters.

1557 The Portuguese set up a trading base at Macao.

1560 Ming forces drive off Mongols and pirate raids, until peace and prosperity are restored.

1575 Spanish begin trade with China.

1592–1598 Ming armies help Koreans to fight off Japanese invaders.

1644 The last Ming emperor, Ssu Tsung, commits suicide.

23

TOKUGAWA JAPAN

The Tokugawa, or Edo, period brought a long period of stability and unity to Japan. In 1603 the emperor appointed Tokugawa Ieyasu to the position of shogun (a powerful military leader and effective ruler of Japan). Ieyasu, the first of the Tokugawa shoguns, ran the country on the emperor's behalf. His government centered on the fishing village of Edo, which later became known as Tokyo. Ieyasu reorganized Japan into regions called domains, each of which was led by a *daimyo* who controlled the local groups of warriors, or samurai.

SAMURAI WARRIORS
Boys trained from childhood to become warriors. Their main weapons were bows and arrows, single-edged swords, and daggers.

The Samurai fought on horseback as well as on foot.

Single-edged sword

Armor for protection

A WARLORD'S STRONGHOLD
*Himeji castle was the stronghold of
the warlord Hideyoshi during the
civil wars that tore Japan apart.*

JAPANESE ISOLATION

At first, Japan was visited
by Portuguese, English, and
Dutch traders. Missionaries
converted many Japanese to Christianity. Ieyasu
thought the new religion might undermine his
rule and in 1637
missionaries were
banned. Despite Japan's
isolation from the rest
of the world the
country flourished
and its population
and food production
increased.

*A complicated
hairstyle made
it difficult to
move the head.*

JAPANESE SOCIETY
*Under the strict society of
the Tokugawas, wealthy
women were treated as
ornaments. The clothing
and shoes they wore
made it almost impossible
to walk.*

Long flowing gown

Very high shoes

1543 Birth of Tokugawa
    Ieyasu.
1560 Ieyasu returns to his
    own lands and allies
    himself with the warlord,
    Nobunaga.
1584 After several small
    battles, Ieyasu allies
    himself with the warlord
    Hideyoshi.
1598 After the death of
    Hideyoshi, Japan's
    warlords struggle for
    power.
1603 The emperor appoints
    Ieyasu shogun and the
    Tokugawa period begins.
1605 Ieyasu abdicates as
    shogun but continues to
    advise his successors.
1616 Death of Ieyasu.
1637 Christianity is banned
    in Japan and foreigners,
    except the Dutch, are
    forced to leave.
1830s Peasants and samurai
    rebel against the
    Tokugawas.
1867 The last Tokugawa
    shogun is overthrown.

THE THIRTY YEARS WAR

The Thirty Years War began in 1618 as a protest by the Protestant noblemen of Bohemia (now part of the Czech Republic) against their Catholic rulers, the Habsburg Holy Roman emperors. The war ended in 1648 with the Treaty of Westphalia, which gave religious freedom and independence to Protestant states. The long war devastated many states in Germany. Some lost more than half their population through disease, famine, and fighting.

SWEDEN AT WAR
Gustavus II Adolphus of Sweden led his troops against the Habsburgs because he believed the Protestant religion was being destroyed.

King Gustavus II Adolphus always fought at the head of his men.

A RELIGIOUS WAR

In 1619 Ferdinand II became Holy Roman emperor but rebellion against his rule soon spread to Germany. In 1620 Ferdinand defeated the Protestant king Frederick and soon Catholicism was the only religion allowed in Bohemia. Spain, also ruled by the Habsburgs, joined the war on the side of the Holy Roman Empire. Believing the Protestant religion to be in danger, the Swedish king Gustavus II Adolphus joined the war against Spain and the Holy Roman Empire. France, although Catholic, also entered the war in order to curtail Habsburg power.

BOHEMIAN PROTEST
The Thirty Years War began after a group of Bohemians threw two Catholics out of a castle window

1618 Thirty Years War starts.

1619 Ferdinand II is crowned Holy Roman emperor.

1620 Ferdinand's army defeats Protestant king Frederick of Bohemia.

1621 Fighting breaks out between Dutch and Spanish in the Rhineland.

1625 Denmark and England join in the war on the side of the Dutch.

1630 King Gustavus II Adolphus of Sweden joins the war on the Protestant side.

1635 Richelieu takes France into the war against the Habsburgs.

1637 French and allies start to defeat Spain.

1648 The Treaty of Westphalia brings an end to the Thirty Years War.

ENGLISH CIVIL WAR

The English Civil War broke out during the reign of Charles I. The king came into regular conflict with parliament, which he dissolved in 1629. For 11 years Charles ruled without parliament's help, but he later recalled it in order to raise money to fight a rebellion in Scotland. When the king tried to arrest five of his opponents in parliament in 1642, civil war broke out. At first the king's forces, or Royalists, were more successful than Parliament's supporters, the Roundheads. Eventually, in 1645, the Roundheads defeated Charles's forces. Charles was found guilty of treason and executed in 1649.

A Roundhead soldier

Preston X   X Marston Moor
Adwalton Moor X   ● YORK

X Naseby

Worcester X   X Edgehill
Cropredy Bridge X
OXFORD ● X Brentford
Bristol X   ●
Roundway Down X   ● LONDON
X Newbury

Lostwithiel
X   ● PLYMOUTH

MAJOR BATTLES
This map shows the main battles of the war. After 1644, the king's forces, the Royalists, held the pink areas. Parliament's soldiers, the Roundheads, controlled the green areas.

Plain woolen jacket

A Royalist soldier

Puritans were strict Protestants who dressed simply and disapproved of theater and dancing.

THE ENGLISH COMMONWEALTH

After Charles's death England became a commonwealth (republic) ruled by parliament. Later, Oliver Cromwell ruled as Lord Protector. His successor, his son Richard, was removed from office. In 1660 Charles I's son returned from exile to reign as Charles II.

DEATH OF THE KING

Charles I was found guilty of treason and executed in January 1649. The execution took place on a scaffold outside the banqueting hall of Whitehall.

Priest

Executioner

Charles I

1625 Charles I comes to the throne.

1629 Parliament tries to curb Charles's power and is dismissed.

1639 Rebellion breaks out in Scotland.

1641 Charles makes peace with the Scots, but rebellion breaks out in Ireland.

1642 Civil war begins. The first major battle takes place at Edgehill, Warwickshire.

1645 The New Model Army, led by Sir Thomas Fairfax and Oliver Cromwell, decisively defeats the Royalists.

1648 Charles starts a second civil war, but is quickly defeated.

1649 Charles is executed on January 31.

1653–1658 Oliver Cromwell rules as Lord Protector.

1660 Restoration of the monarchy; Charles II comes to the throne.

NAPOLEON

Napoleon Bonaparte made his name in the French army, rising to become the Emperor of France. He became an officer at the age of 16, and won his first victory against rebels during the French Revolution. In 1798 the French army, under Napoleon, defeated the Egyptians and the Ottomans, but the French navy was itself defeated by the British at the battle of the Nile. Napoleon overthrew the *Directoire*, or committee, that ruled France and in 1804 he proclaimed himself Emperor.

THE BATTLE OF AUSTERLITZ
In December 1805, a French army of 73,000, under the command of Napoleon and his generals, defeated an army of 87,000 Austrians and Russians. The enemy was lured into a valley where many were killed.

THE CODE NAPOLEON
Napoleon introduced a code of laws that incorporated many of the ideas of the French Revolution.

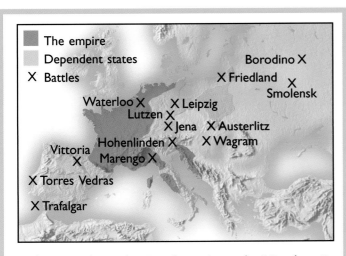

This map shows the French empire under Napoleon I and the dependent states that were virtually part of it. The main battles of the Napoleonic Wars are also shown

THE NAPOLEONIC WARS

Napoleon was a brilliant general who commanded thousands of conscripted men. In 1805 the British, under Lord Nelson, defeated the French fleet at Trafalgar. On land, Napoleon seemed undefeatable, but in 1812 his invasion of Russia was disastrous and his army in Spain suffered setbacks. After abdicating in 1814, he raised a new army the following year. Napoleon was defeated at the battle of Waterloo.

1769 Birth of Napoleon at Ajaccio, Corsica.

1795 Napoleon defends Paris against rebels.

1798 Nelson defeats the French fleet at the battle of the Nile, Egypt.

1802 Napoleon plans to invade Britain.

1803 Britain declares war on France.

1804 Napoleon declares himself emperor of France.

1805 Nelson defeats French fleet at Trafalgar. Napoleon defeats the Austrians and Russians at the battle of Austerlitz.

1812 Napoleon's army invades Russia but is defeated by the harsh climate.

1814 Napoleon is forced to abdicate and is exiled.

1815 Napoleon raises a new army. He is defeated at the battle of Waterloo.

1821 Napoleon dies in exile.

SOUTH AMERICA

In the early nineteenth century Spain and Portugal still ruled vast colonies in South America, but the colonists had begun to fight for their independence. The main struggle against Spanish rule was led by Simón Bolívar from Venezuela and José de San Martin from Argentina. San Martin gained freedom for his country in 1816, but Bolívar's fight was longer and more difficult. He joined a rebel army that captured Caracas, capital of Venezuela, in 1810, but was defeated by the Spanish. Bolívar became the army's leader but was defeated by the Spanish again.

THE BATTLE OF AYACHUCHO
At the battle of Ayachucho in 1824, Simón Bolívar's army defeated the Spanish. He had finally secured independence for Peru. Part of the newly liberated Peru became the republic of Bolivia, named for Bolívar.

JOSÉ DE SAN MARTIN
José de San Martin freed Argentina from Spanish rule. He then led his army over the Andes mountains to help the Chilean people gain their independence.

FREEDOM FROM SPANISH RULE

In 1819, Bolívar led his army over the Andes into Colombia and defeated the Spanish in a surprise attack. He later freed Venezuela, Ecuador, and Panama from Spanish rule, making them part of the Republic of Gran Colombia. Bolívar became president of the new state.

BOLIVIANS TODAY
Today, Bolivians wear dress that combines ancient patterns with Spanish influences.

1808 Independence struggles begin in South America.

1816 José de San Martin leads Argentina to independence from Spain.

1817 At the battle of Chacabuco in Chile, San Martin and Bernado O'Higgins are victorious over the Spanish.

1818 Chile becomes independent from Spain.

1819 Simón Bolívar defeats the Spanish at the battle of Boyoca. Colombia wins independence from Spain.

1821 Bolívar's victory over the Spanish at Carabobo ensures independence for Venezuela.

1822 Brazil wins independence from Portugal.

1824 Bolívar wins independence for Peru.

1825 Bolivia is named for Bolívar.

1828 Uruguay wins independence from Spain.

33

AMERICAN CIVIL WAR

In the United States, by the early nineteenth century, industry and trade had developed in the North. In the South, agriculture and slavery dominated. When Abraham Lincoln, who opposed slavery, was elected president, 11 southern states formed their own Confederacy. This marked the beginning of the Civil War.

ULYSSES S. GRANT
Grant commanded the Union armies and led them to victory.

THE BATTLE OF BULL RUN

The battle of Bull Run, Virginia, in 1861 was the first major battle of the Civil War. Confederate forces defeated the Union army.

Union soldiers wore blue uniforms.

Cannon mounted on wheels.

Confederate forces wore gray uniforms.

GENERAL ROBERT E. LEE
Although Lee's Confederate forces were defeated, he was an outstanding leader.

NORTH VERSUS SOUTH

The North had more soldiers and more money, and the industry to provide weapons. It controlled the navy and was able to blockade southern ports, preventing the South from exporting cotton and getting supplies from abroad. The South won the early battles of the war, but in 1863, the war turned in the North's favor when Unionist troops defeated Confederate forces at Gettysburg, Pennsylvania. Lincoln announced his aim to abolish slavery throughout the United States. By the time the Confederates surrendered in 1865, much of the South lay in ruins.

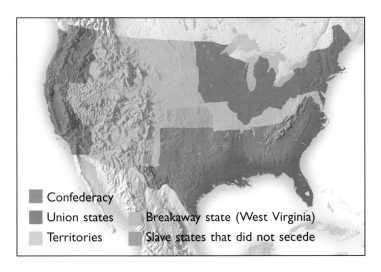

- Confederacy
- Union states
- Territories
- Breakaway state (West Virginia)
- Slave states that did not secede

1861 Civil War starts when Confederate troops attack the Union garrison at Fort Sumter, South Carolina. Confederates win the battle of Bull Run, Virginia.

1862 Confederate general Lee prevents Union army taking Richmond, Virginia and defeats another Union army at Fredericksburg, Virginia.

1863 Emancipation Proclamation is signed. Lee is defeated at Gettysburg, Pennsylvania. Grant's Union army captures Vicksburg, Mississippi.

1864 Union forces besiege Confederates at Petersburg, Virginia.

1865 Grant's forces capture Richmond, Virginia. On April 9, Lee surrenders to Grant, bringing the war to an end. On April 15, President Lincoln is assassinated by Confederate sympathizer John Wilkes Booth.

WORLD WAR I

By the late 1800s, Germany had become a major industrial and military power and France and Britain in particular felt threatened by this. Germany formed the Triple Alliance with Austria–Hungary and Italy, while Britain, France, and Russia formed the Triple Entente. Both Britain and Germany enlarged their navies, and all Europe's armies were expanding. In 1914, the assassination by a Serbian citizen of Archduke Franz Ferdinand, heir to the Austro-Hungarian throne, sparked off the war.

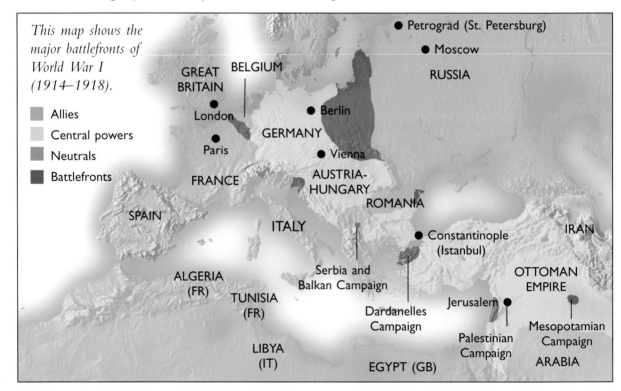

This map shows the major battlefronts of World War I (1914–1918).

Allies
Central powers
Neutrals
Battlefronts

Petrograd (St. Petersburg)
Moscow
RUSSIA
GREAT BRITAIN
BELGIUM
London
Berlin
GERMANY
Paris
Vienna
AUSTRIA-HUNGARY
FRANCE
ROMANIA
SPAIN
ITALY
Constantinople (Istanbul)
IRAN
Serbia and Balkan Campaign
ALGERIA (FR)
OTTOMAN EMPIRE
TUNISIA (FR)
Dardanelles Campaign
Jerusalem
Palestinian Campaign
Mesopotamian Campaign
LIBYA (IT)
EGYPT (GB)
ARABIA

THE FIRST TANKS
Making their first appearance in battle in 1916, tanks helped to break the stalemate of trench warfare.

THE GREAT WAR

Following the 1914 assassination, Austria–Hungary declared war on Serbia, and Russia mobilized its army to defend Serbia. Germany declared war on Russia and France. Britain joined the war to defend Belgium from German attack. The Great War involved two groups of countries—the Allies (France, Britain, Russia, Italy, Japan, and the United States) and the Central Powers (Germany, Austria–Hungary, and Turkey).

WAR LEADERS
The Allied war leaders led their countries to victory. The United States joined the war in April 1917.

David Lloyd George (Britain)   *Georges Clemenceau (France)*

Woodrow Wilson, President of the United States

1882 Germany, Austria–Hungary and Italy form the Triple Alliance to defend each other if there is a war.

1891 France and Russia agree that, if either is attacked, the other will give full military support.

1907 Russia joins with Britain and France to form the Triple Entente.

1914 June 28, Archduke Franz Ferdinand is assassinated by a Serbian protester in Sarajevo.

July 28 Austria declares war on Serbia.

August 1 Germany declares war on Russia to defend Austria.

August 3 Germany declares war on France, Russia's ally.

August 4 German armies march through Belgium to France. Britain declares war on Germany. World War I begins.

37

IN THE TRENCHES

Most of World War I was fought from two parallel lines of trenches separated by a short stretch of "no-man's land." This trench warfare was necessary because the power, speed and accuracy of the weapons used on both sides made it impossible to fight a battle in the open. When soldiers did go over the top of their trenches to launch an attack, often only a few yards of ground were gained and the cost in casualties was enormous.

LIFE IN THE TRENCHES
Soldiers slept and ate in their trenches, which were usually cold, muddy, and wet.

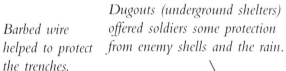

Life in the trenches was miserable.

Barbed wire helped to protect the trenches.

Dugouts (underground shelters) offered soldiers some protection from enemy shells and the rain.

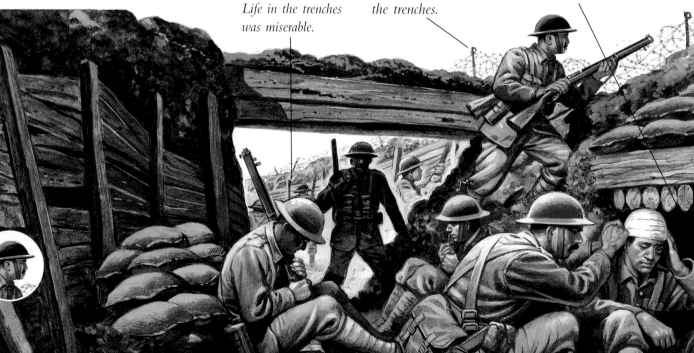

*German Fokker
E1 monoplane*

Sopwith Camel

WORLD WAR I PLANES
At first, planes spied on enemy trenches and troop movements. Later, they were used in aerial combat and in bombing raids.

THE ARMISTICE
In 1917, Russia started peace talks with Germany. By September 1918 over 1,200,000 well-equipped US soldiers joined the Allied forces. By October, almost all German-occupied France and part of Belgium had been reclaimed, and Turkey and Austria were defeated. On November 11 Germany and the Allies signed an armistice, ending World War I.

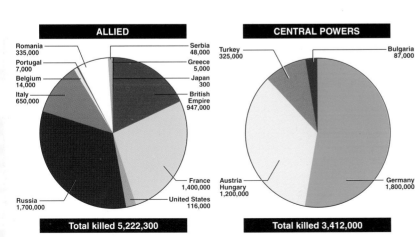

ALLIED

Romania 335,000
Portugal 7,000
Belgium 14,000
Italy 650,000
Russia 1,700,000
Serbia 48,000
Greece 5,000
Japan 300
British Empire 947,000
France 1,400,000
United States 116,000

Total killed 5,222,300

CENTRAL POWERS

Turkey 325,000
Austria Hungary 1,200,000
Bulgaria 87,000
Germany 1,800,000

Total killed 3,412,000

1915 British naval blockade of Germany leads to a German submarine blockade of Britain.

April–May Germany uses poison gas for first time.

1916 Battle for Verdun, France, lasts five months.

July 1 Start of the battle of the Somme.

1917 US joins the war on Allied side.

1918 March 3, Russia and Germany sign armistice.

July Germans launch offensive on the Western Front.

August Allies force Germans to retreat.

October Austria–Hungary surrenders.

November Armistice is signed on November 11 at 11 o'clock. World War I ends.

1919 Treaty of Versailles orders Germany to pay large amounts of compensation to its former enemies.

TROUBLE IN IRELAND

At the end of World War I, the question of Irish independence from Britain became critical. Most people in the six northern counties, known as Ulster, wanted to remain part of Britain, while in the south most wanted Ireland to become an independent republic. Conflict between the two sides pushed Ireland to the brink of civil war, only prevented by the outbreak of World War I. On Easter Monday, 1916, an armed rebellion declared Ireland a republic. After four days of fighting the protesters surrendered.

THE EASTER RISING

The Easter Rising of 1916 saw fighting on the streets of Dublin between British soldiers and Irish Republicans. Around 100 British soldiers and 450 Irish Republicans and civilians were killed.

Irish Republicans

British soldiers

Barricades were set up in the streets.

THE REPUBLICAN STRUGGLE

In 1918, newly elected Sinn Fein MPs set up their own parliament in Dublin. The Anglo-Irish Treaty of 1921 made most of Ireland independent, leaving Northern Ireland under British rule. Civil war between supporters of the treaty and the Republicans ended when, in 1923, the Republicans accepted the division of Ireland for the time being.

EAMON DE VALERA
(1882–1975)
American-born Eamon de Valera took part in the Easter Rising of 1916. In 1932, his Fianna Fail political party won the Irish general election and he served as head of government for many years.

1886–1893 Attempts to give Ireland its own parliament are defeated.

1896 The Irish Socialist and Republican Party is founded.

1905 Sinn Fein, the Irish nationalist party, is founded.

1912 Outbreak of World War I prevents the enactment of the third Irish Home Rule bill.

1916 Irish Republicans in Dublin in armed revolt against British rule.

1918 Sinn Fein MPs set up their own parliament in Dublin.

1919 Outbreak of fighting between British troops and Irish Republicans.

1921 Anglo-Irish Treaty separates Ulster from the rest of Ireland.

1922 Outbreak of civil war between supporters of the Anglo-Irish Treaty and its opponents.

1937 The Irish Free State becomes Eire.

1949 Eire becomes the Republic of Ireland.

41

REVOLUTION IN CHINA

 China became a republic in 1911 when the Kuomintang, the Chinese Nationalist Party, overthrew the Manchu Dynasty. When Chiang Kai-shek became Kuomintang leader in 1925, the Chinese Communist Party had already been founded. Civil war broke out between the two parties in 1927.

The Kuomintang claimed to govern the whole of China, but the Communists, under Mao Zedong, established a rival government in Jiangxi province. In 1933 Chiang Kai-shek attacked the Communists. In order to escape, Mao led 100,000 Communists on the "Long March." At its end he became Communist leader.

The Long March from Jiangxi to Shaanxi took 568 days and claimed around 80,000 lives.

About 100,000 marchers set off on the long journey.

The march covered about 6,000 miles.

Mao Zedong led the marchers.

COMMUNIST VICTORY

When the Japanese invaded China in 1937, the Kuomintang and the Communists united to defeat them. But in 1945 civil war broke out again. The Communists defeated the Kuomintang, forcing them off the Chinese mainland and onto the island of Taiwan. On October 1, 1949, mainland China became the People's Republic of China.

Mao Zedong (1893–1976)

THE LONG MARCH
This map shows the route taken on the Long March from 1934 to 1935.

1905 Sun Yat-sen founds the Kuomintang (Chinese Nationalist Party).

1911 Collapse of the Manchu Empire. Sun Yat-sen becomes president.

1921 Foundation of the Chinese Communist party. Mao Zedong is one of its first members.

1925 Chiang Kai-shek succeeds Sun Yat-sen as leader of China.

1927 Start of civil war between the Communists and the Kuomintang.

1933 Chiang Kai-shek attacks the Communists in Jiangxi.

1934 Mao leads Communists on the "Long March."

1935 Mao becomes leader of the Communist Party.

1937–1945 The Kuomintang and Communists unite to fight against Japan.

1946 Civil war breaks out again.

1949 The People's Republic of China is proclaimed.

WORLD WAR II

World War II started on September 3, 1939, two days after Adolf Hitler's troops invaded Poland. The war was fought between the Axis powers (Germany, Italy, and Japan) and the Allies (Britain and the Commonwealth countries, France, the United States, the Soviet Union, and China). The Germans' tactics became known as the *Blitzkrieg* ("lightning war"). They made surprise tank attacks and overcame the opposition quickly. By June 1940, most of Europe had fallen.

AIR RAIDS
The bombing of cities and towns killed and injured many thousands of civilians on both sides.

THE BATTLE OF BRITAIN
The battle of Britain was fought in the skies above southeast England in 1940. Britain had far fewer planes than Germany but managed to win.

THE WAR CONTINUES

In 1940 Hitler's air force, the Luftwaffe, attacked southern England, trying to crush morale and destroy the British air force. The Germans were defeated, preventing Hitler's planned invasion of Britain. Hitler invaded his former ally, the Soviet Union, in June 1941. In December 1941, the United States joined the war following Japan's attack on Pearl Harbor in Hawaii.

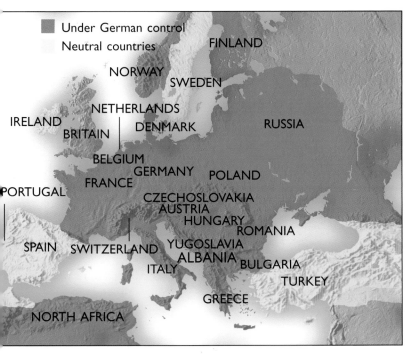

GERMAN CONTROL
By the end of 1941 the continent of Europe was almost completely under German control.

1939 Germany annexes Czechoslovakia. Italy annexes Albania. Italian/German alliance.

August 23 Germany and USSR sign non-aggression pact.

August 25 British, French and Polish alliance.

September 1 Germany invades Poland.

September 3 Britain and France declare war on Germany.

September 17 USSR invades Poland.

1940 March USSR takes Finland. German submarines attack British merchant ships.

April–May Germany occupies Norway, Denmark, Belgium, and the Netherlands.

June Germany occupies France. Allies evacuate from Dunkirk.

August–October Battle of Britain.

November Italy tries to invade Greece.

45

THE WORLD AT WAR

By May 1942 Japan had control of Southeast Asia as well as many Pacific islands. By August the US had defeated Japan's navy, stopping them from invading further territory. British troops led by Field-Marshall Montgomery won a decisive battle at El Alamein, Egypt, in 1942. The Allies in North Africa forced the Axis armies to surrender. German troops in the Soviet Union also faced great difficulties. In 1943 the Russians defeated the Germans at the battle of Stalingrad, with many lives lost on both sides.

Field-Marshall Montgomery

Roosevelt and Churchill in Casablanca in 1943.

Hirohito, Emperor of Japan

WAR LEADERS
Montgomery defeated the Germans at El Alamein in 1942. De Gaulle was leader of the resistance movement in France. Roosevelt and Churchill met in 1943 to discuss the war's progress. The Japanese emperor's powers were diminished after Japan's defeat.

Heinrich Himmler, head of the Nazi SS

46

THE ALLIED INVASION

By July 2, 1944 one million Allied troops had landed in France and were advancing toward Germany. In April 1945 they reached the Ruhr, center of German manufacturing and arms production. Hitler committed suicide in Berlin on April 30. Soviet troops captured Berlin, and on May 7 Germany surrendered.

Charles de Gaulle

THE SIEGE OF LENINGRAD
German and Finnish forces besieged the Soviet city of Leningrad from September 1941 to January 1944.

1941 February Allies capture 113,000 Italian soldiers in North Africa.

April Yugoslavia and Greece fall to Germany.

May German invasion of USSR begins.

December 7 Japan attacks Pearl Harbor. The United States declares war on Japan. Italy and Germany declare war on the United States.

December Japan invades Malaya and Hong Kong.

1942 February Singapore falls to the Japanese; 90,000 British and Commonwealth troops are taken prisoner.

May The Philippines and Burma fall to the Japanese.

August US victory at the battle of Guadalcanal ends Japanese expansion. The battle of Stalingrad begins.

October In North Africa, Allies defeat Axis forces at the battle of El Alamein, Egypt.

THE WAR ENDS

After the end of the war in Europe, fighting continued in Asia. In September 1944, US troops invaded the Philippines, while the British led a campaign to reconquer Burma. The US dropped an atomic bomb on Hiroshima, in Japan, on August 6, 1945. Three days later a second atomic bomb was dropped on Nagasaki. Thousands of people died, and many thousands more died later from radiation sickness, and other injuries. Five days later, the Japanese government surrendered and on August 14, World War II ended.

ATOMIC BLAST
The atomic bombs that were dropped on Nagasaki (above) and Hiroshima totally devastated the two cities.

D-DAY
The Allied invasion of Europe began on June 6, 1944 (known as D-Day). Around 156,000 troops were landed on the beaches of Normandy, in France, in the largest seaborne attack ever mounted.

Allied soldiers landed on five different beaches in Normandy.

The troops stormed ashore, often under heavy enemy fire.

Landing craft

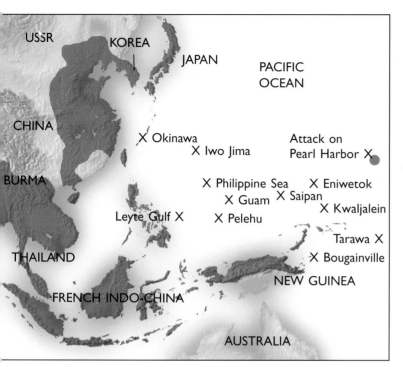

WAR IN THE PACIFIC
*By 1942, Japan held all the orange areas on the map.
The crosses mark the ensuing battles in the Pacific.*

WAR CASUALTIES

The loss of life from fighting was enormous, and others died through ill treatment as prisoners of war. Millions of civilians died through bombing raids or through illness and starvation. Around six million Jewish people died in concentration camps. After the war, leading Nazis were tried for war crimes and crimes against humanity.

1943 February The Germans are defeated at the battle of Stalingrad.

May Axis troops in North Africa surrender.

July Mussolini is overthrown and Italy declares war on Germany.

1944 June Allied forces land in Normandy, France.

October Allies invade Philippines.

December Start of battle of the Bulge, last German offensive.

1945 February Yalta Conference.

March US forces capture Iwo Jima.

April Hitler commits suicide.

May Soviet troops enter Berlin. Germany surrenders.

July Potsdam Conference agrees division of Germany.

August Japan surrenders after atomic bombs are dropped on Hiroshima and Nagasaki.

49

THE COLD WAR

Although the United States and the Soviet Union were allies in World War II, soon afterwards they became enemies in what was called the Cold War. The Soviet Union set up communist governments in Eastern Europe. To stop communism spreading to the West, the US-backed Marshall Plan gave money to countries whose economies had been ruined by the war. In 1948 the Soviets blockaded West Berlin (the city lay inside Soviet-controlled territory, but was divided between the Allies). The blockade was defeated, and the following year Germany was divided into West and East.

*Symbol of the
United Nations*

*A DIVIDED EUROPE
This map shows how
Europe was divided after
World War II. The
boundary between the two
halves of Europe was
known as the "iron
curtain." Few people
crossed this divide.*

NATO countries
Warsaw Pact
Neutral countries

FINLAND
NORWAY
SWEDEN
NETHERLANDS
DENMARK
RUSSIA
IRELAND
BRITAIN
EAST
BELGIUM GERMANY POLAND
LUXEMBOURG WEST
GERMANY CZECHOSLOVAKIA
FRANCE
AUSTRIA
HUNGARY
ROMANIA
PORTUGAL
YUGOSLAVIA
SPAIN SWITZERLAND BULGARIA
ITALY ALBANIA
TURKEY
GREECE

NATO

In 1949 the countries of Western Europe and North America formed a military alliance known as the North Atlantic Treaty Organization (NATO).

Symbol of NATO

THE CUBAN CRISIS

Both the United States and the Soviet Union began stockpiling nuclear weapons. In 1962, the Soviet Union built missile bases in Cuba that threatened the United States. The US Navy blockaded Cuba and eventually the Soviets removed the missiles.

Soviet troops

Tanks blocked the streets of Prague.

THE INVASION OF PRAGUE
Soviet tanks entered Prague, Czechoslovakia's capital, in August 1968. A liberal government had introduced many reforms, which worried the Soviets.

1947 US-backed Marshall Plan gives financial aid to European countries.

1948 Blockade of West Berlin by the Soviet Union.

1949 NATO formed. The Soviets explode their first atomic warhead.

1955 Warsaw Pact formed among countries of Eastern Europe.

1956 Soviets invade Hungary to preserve communist rule.

1961 The Berlin Wall is built.

1962 Cuban missile crisis.

1963 The United States and Soviet Union sign Nuclear Test-Ban Treaty.

1964 The United States becomes involved in the Vietnam War.

1968 Soviet Union invades Czechoslovakia to preserve communist rule.

1979 Afghanistan is invaded by the Soviet Union.

1983 The United States invades Grenada.

THE VIETNAM WAR

Vietnam, Cambodia, and Laos made up the French colony of Indochina. During World War II Vietnam declared its independence. War broke out between the French and Vietnamese, ending in French defeat in 1954. Vietnam was divided into communist North and noncommunist South, but civil war broke out between the two countries. From 1959, communist guerrillas in the South, known as the Viet Cong, were helped by North Vietnam.

VILLAGE LIFE
Many Vietnamese civilians suffered greatly in the war as their crops and villages were destroyed to flush out and kill the Viet Cong soldiers.

SUPPLY ROUTE
The Viet Cong brought their supplies along the Ho Chi Minh trail, from China through Laos into South Vietnam.

HO CHI MINH (1892–1969)
Ho Chi Minh led Vietnam in its
struggle for independence from France.
Later, he fought for a united Vietnam.

JUNGLE WARFARE

The United States sent
troops to help the South from 1965. In order
to cut off supply lines, US planes bombed
North Vietnam. Villages and jungle areas of
South Vietnam were sprayed with chemicals to
destroy Viet Cong hiding places. In 1969, after
a Viet Cong offensive, the United States began
to withdraw its troops. A cease-fire was agreed
in 1973.

Most Vietnamese were
farmers. They grew rice in the
fields around their villages.

1946 Start of the war
between Vietnamese
nationalists and French
colonial troops.

1954 Vietnamese communists
defeat the French at
Dien Bien Phu. The
country is divided into
North Vietnam and
South Vietnam.

1963 South Vietnamese
government is
overthrown.

1964 War breaks out between
North and South
Vietnam.

1965 US troops arrive in
South Vietnam.

1968 North Vietnamese and
Viet Cong offensive.

1969 25,000 of 540,000 US
troops are withdrawn.

1972 Peace talks start again.

1973 A cease-fire is agreed—
US troops withdraw.

1975 The communists take
control of Vietnam.

1976 Vietnam is reunited
under a communist
government.

53

MIDDLE EAST CRISIS

An uneasy peace followed Israel's defeat of the Arab League in 1948. Large numbers of Jews continued to migrate to Israel from overseas. The Palestinian Arabs began to campaign for a land of their own. In 1956 Britain and France fought Egypt over control of the Suez Canal. Israel felt threatened and invaded Egypt's Sinai Peninsula, destroying bases there. In the Six Day War in June 1967, Israel took control of all Jerusalem, the West Bank, the Golan Heights, the Gaza Strip, and Sinai. In 1973 Egyptian and Syrian forces attacked Israel but were defeated.

BEIRUT DESTROYED
Large parts of Beirut, the capital of Lebanon, were destroyed by fighting which began in 1976.

THE PEACE PROCESS
At peace talks in 1993, Israeli prime minister Yitzhak Rabin and Yasser Arafat, leader of the Palestinian Liberation Organization, guided by US President Clinton, agreed in principle to limited Palestinian self-rule.

President Clinton

Yasser Arafat

Yitzhak Rabin

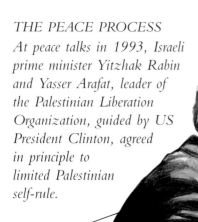

AYATOLLAH KHOMEINI
(1900–1989)
Khomeini, a religious leader of Iran, came to power in 1979. He changed Iran into a strictly Muslim state.

WAR AND PEACE

In 1980 war broke out between the oil-producing countries of Iraq and Iran. In 1990 Iraqi troops invaded Kuwait but were defeated by UN forces. Peace agreements have been signed between Israel and Egypt, Jordan, and Syria, but tension and conflict continue to disrupt the peace process.

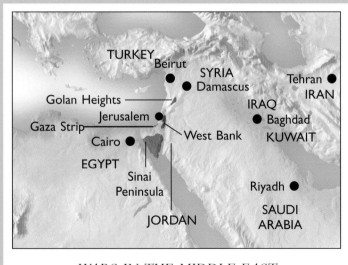

WARS IN THE MIDDLE EAST
The shaded area shows land taken by Israel in the 1967 Six Day War.

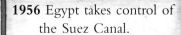

1956 Egypt takes control of the Suez Canal.

1964 Formation of the Palestinian Liberation Organization (PLO).

1967 Six Day War, between Israel and Egypt, Jordan and Syria, is won by Israel.

1973 Yom Kippur War between Israel and Egypt and Syria.

1976 Fighting breaks out in Lebanon.

1979 Peace treaty between Israel and Egypt. Islamic republican government is set up in Iran.

1980–1988 Iran–Iraq War.

1982 Israel invades Lebanon.

1990–1991 The Gulf War.

1993 Israeli and Palestinian peace talks.

1994 Israel and Jordan sign a peace agreement.

1995 Israel extends limited self-rule to the Palestinians.

55

THE COLD WAR FADES

In the early 1960s, the United States and the Soviet Union remained deeply suspicious of each other. Tension between them eased a little with the signing of two agreements to reduce the arms race. However, when Ronald Reagan, an extreme anti-communist, became US president in 1981, he increased military spending. In 1985 the new Soviet leader, Mikhail Gorbachev, introduced reforms, lessening tension between the superpowers. Two years later, Gorbachev and Reagan signed an agreement banning medium-range nuclear missiles.

CZECHS REVOLT
Czechoslovakians demonstrate in the capital Prague in 1989, demanding greater democracy without fear of recriminations.

THE COLLAPSE OF COMMUNISM

Demolishing the Berlin Wall

Gorbachev's reforms led to demands for free elections in Eastern Europe and by the end of 1989, communism had collapsed in Poland, Hungary, East Germany, Czechoslovakia and Romania. In the following year, East and West Germany were reunited for the first time since 1945. In 1991 the Soviet Union was abolished, losing its superpower status. The Cold War had finally ended.

GORBACHEV'S REFORMS
Gorbachev opened the Soviet Union to Western enterprise, encouraging companies such as McDonald's to open up in his country.

1967 The United States, Britain, and the Soviet Union ban the use of nuclear weapons in outer space.

1972 The first Strategic Arms Limitation Talks (SALT) agreement is signed by the US and the Soviet Union.

1979 Second SALT agreement is signed.

1981 Reagan increases US military spending.

1985 Gorbachev makes reforms in the Soviet Union.

1989 Free elections held in Poland. Communism collapses in Hungary, East Germany, Czechoslovakia and Romania. The Berlin Wall is demolished.

1990 East and West Germany are reunited. Free elections are held in Bulgaria.

1991 Albania has a multiparty government. The Soviet Union is replaced by 15 independent nations.

57

IMPORTANT BATTLES OF HISTORY

Marathon (490 B.C.) The armies of Athens crushed an attempt by Persia to conquer Greece

Salamis (480 B.C.) Greek ships defeated a larger Persian fleet and thwarted an invasion

Syracuse (414–413 B.C.) During a long war between the city states of Athens and Sparta the Athenians besieged Syracuse but lost power after a heavy defeat

Gaugamela (331 B.C.) Alexander the Great of Macedonia defeated the Persians and conquered the Persian Empire

Metaurus (207 B.C.) A Roman army defeated a Carthaginian attempt to invade Italy

Actium (30 B.C.) A Roman fleet destroyed the Egyptian fleet of Mark Antony and Cleopatra, ending Egypt's threat to Rome

Teutoburg Forest (A.D. 9) German tribes led by Arminius ambushed and destroyed three Roman legions

Châlons (451) Roman legions and their Visigoth allies defeated the Huns, led by Attila

Poitiers (732) The Franks led by Charles Martel defeated a Muslim attempt to conquer western Europe

Hastings (1066) Duke William of Normandy defeated the Saxons under King Harold II and conquered England

Crécy (1346) Edward III of England defeated Philip VI of France, using archers to shoot his opponents

Agincourt (1415) Henry V of England defeated a much larger French army and captured Normandy

Orléans (1429) The French under Joan of Arc raised the siege of Orléans and began liberating France from England

Constantinople (1453) Ottoman Turks captured the city and ended the Byzantine (Eastern Roman) Empire

Lepanto (1571) A Christian fleet defeated a Turkish fleet in the Mediterranean and halted Muslim designs on Europe

Spanish Armada (1588) England fought off a Spanish attempt to invade and conquer it

Naseby (1645) Parliamentary forces defeated Charles I, leading to the end of the English Civil War

Blenheim (1704) During the War of the Spanish Succession, British and Austrian forces stopped a French and Bavarian attempt to capture Vienna

Poltava (1709) Peter the Great of Russia fought off an invasion by Charles XII of Sweden

Plassey (1757) An Anglo-Indian army defeated the Nawab of Bengal, beginning England's domination of India

Quebec (1759) British troops under James Wolfe defeated the French and secured Canada for Britain

Bunker Hill (1775) In the War of Independence, British troops drove the Americans from hills near Boston, Massachusetts

Brandywine Creek (1777) British troops forced American forces to retreat

Saratoga (1777) American troops surrounded a British army and forced it to surrender

Savannah (1778) Britain captured the port of Savannah from the Americans and gained control of Georgia

King's Mountain (1780) Americans surrounded and captured part of a British army

Yorktown (1781) A British army surrendered to a larger American force, ending the American War of Independence

The Nile (1798) A British fleet shattered a French fleet in Abu Kir Bay, ending Napoleon's attempt to conquer Egypt

Trafalgar (1805) A British fleet defeated a Franco-Spanish fleet, ending Napoleon's hopes of invading England

Austerlitz (1805) Napoleon I of France defeated a combined force of Austrian and Russian soldiers

Leipzig (1813) Austrian, Prussian, Russian and Swedish armies defeated Napoleon I, leading to his abdication the following year

Waterloo (1815) A British, Belgian, and Dutch army supported by the Prussians defeated Napoleon I, ending his brief return to power in France

Fort Sumter (1861) In the opening battle of the American Civil War, Confederate forces captured this fort in the harbor of Charleston, South Carolina

Merrimack and Monitor (1862) This inconclusive battle was the first between two ironclad warships

Gettysburg (1863) Union forces defeated the Confederates, marking a turning point in the American Civil War

Vicksburg (1863) After a long siege Union forces captured this key city on the Mississippi River

Chickamauga (1863) At this town in Georgia the Confederates won their last major battle

Chattanooga (1863) A few weeks after Chickamauga, Union forces won a decisive victory over the Confederates

Tsushima (1905) A Japanese fleet overwhelmed a Russian one, ending the Russo-Japanese War

Tannenberg (1914) At the start of World War I two Russian armies invaded East Prussia, but a German army under Paul von Hindenburg crushed them

Marne (1914) The French and British halted a German invasion of France at the start of World War I

1st Ypres (1914) A series of German attacks on this Belgian town were beaten back with heavy losses on each side

2nd Ypres (1915) The Germans attacked again with heavy shelling and chlorine gas, but gained only a little ground

Isonzo (1916–1917) This was a series of 11 inconclusive battles on the Italo-Austrian front

Verdun (1916) French forces under Philippe Pétain fought off a German attempt to take this strong point

Jutland (1916) This was the major naval battle of World War I; neither Germans nor British won

Brusilov Offensive (1916) A Russian attack led by General Alexei Brusilov nearly knocked Germany's Austrian allies out of the war

Somme (1916) A British and French attack was beaten back by German machine-gunners; total casualties for both sides were more than 1 million

3rd Ypres (1917) British and Canadian troops attacked to drive the Germans back, fighting in heavy rain and mud

Passchendaele (1917) This village was the furthest advance of 3rd Ypres; casualties of both sides totalled 500,000

4th Ypres (1918) This was part of a general German offensive, which died down after heavy fighting

Marne (1918) French, American, and British forces halted the last German attack of World War I

Britain (1940–1941) In World War II, German attempt to eliminate Britain's air force failed

The Atlantic (1940–1944) Germany narrowly lost the submarine war against Allied shipping

Pearl Harbor (1941) In a surprise air attack Japan knocked out the United States fleet at Hawaii

Coral Sea (1942) In the first all-air naval battle, Americans thwarted a Japanese attack on New Guinea

Stalingrad (1942–1943) The German siege of Stalingrad (now Volgograd, Russia) ended with the surrender of a German army of 100,000 men

El Alamein (1942) The British Eighth Army finally drove German and Italian forces out of Egypt

Midway (1942) An American fleet defeated a Japanese attempt to capture Midway Island in the Pacific

Normandy (1944) American and British troops landed in occupied France to begin the defeat of Germany; the largest ever seaborne attack

Leyte Gulf (1944) In the biggest naval battle of World War II, an American fleet thwarted a Japanese attempt to prevent the recapture of the Philippines

Ardennes Bulge (1944–1945) A final German attempt to counter the Allied invasion failed

Hiroshima/Nagasaki (1945) Two US atomic bombs on these cities knocked Japan out of World War II

Falklands (1982) A British seaborne assault recaptured the Falkland Islands following an Argentine invasion

Desert Storm (1991) An American, British, and Arab attack ended Iraq's invasion of Kuwait

INDEX

ACKNOWLEDGMENTS

The publishers wish to thank the following artists who have
contributed to this book.

Martin Camm, Richard Hook, Rob Jakeway, John James, Shane
Marsh, Roger Payne, Mark Peppé, Eric Rowe, Peter Sarson,
Roger Smith, Michael Welply, and Michael White.

All other photographs from the Miles Kelly Archive.